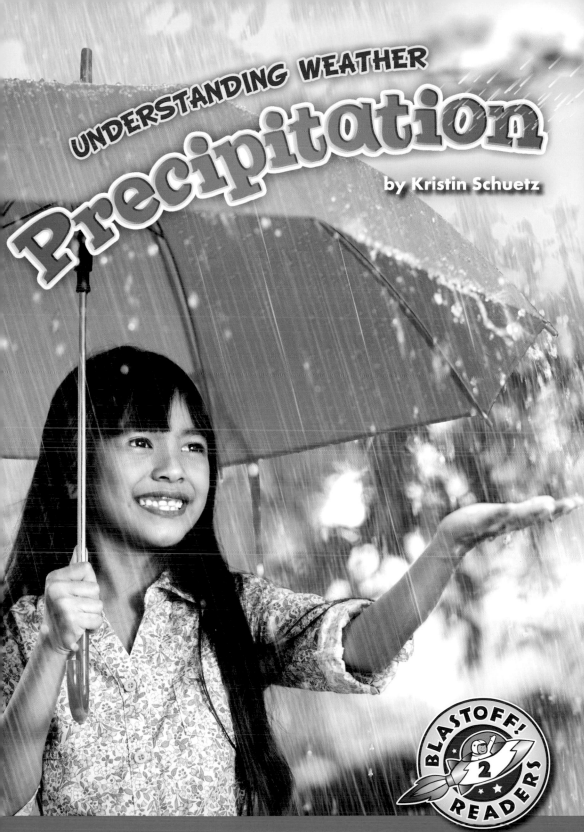

UNDERSTANDING WEATHER

Precipitation

by Kristin Schuetz

BELLWETHER MEDIA • MINNEAPOLIS, MN

Note to Librarians, Teachers, and Parents:

Blastoff! Readers are carefully developed by literacy experts and combine standards-based content with developmentally appropriate text.

Level 1 provides the most support through repetition of high-frequency words, light text, predictable sentence patterns, and strong visual support.

Level 2 offers early readers a bit more challenge through varied simple sentences, increased text load, and less repetition of high-frequency words.

Level 3 advances early-fluent readers toward fluency through increased text and concept load, less reliance on visuals, longer sentences, and more literary language.

Level 4 builds reading stamina by providing more text per page, increased use of punctuation, greater variation in sentence patterns, and increasingly challenging vocabulary.

Level 5 encourages children to move from "learning to read" to "reading to learn" by providing even more text, varied writing styles, and less familiar topics.

Whichever book is right for your reader, Blastoff! Readers are the perfect books to build confidence and encourage a love of reading that will last a lifetime!

This edition first published in 2016 by Bellwether Media, Inc.

No part of this publication may be reproduced in whole or in part without written permission of the publisher. For information regarding permission, write to Bellwether Media, Inc., Attention: Permissions Department, 5357 Penn Avenue South, Minneapolis, MN 55419.

Library of Congress Cataloging-in-Publication Data

Schuetz, Kristin, author.
  Precipitation / by Kristin Schuetz.
    pages cm – (Blastoff! readers: understanding weather)
  Summary: "Developed by literacy experts for students in kindergarten through grade three, this book introduces precipitation to young readers through leveled text and related photos"–Provided by publisher.
  Includes bibliographical references and index.
  Audience: 5-8.
  Audience: K to Grade 3.
  ISBN 978-1-62617-253-1 (hardcover : alk. paper)
  1. Precipitation (Meteorology)–Juvenile iiterature. I. Title.
  QC920.S35 2016
  551.57'7–dc23
                        2015006543

Printed in the United States of America, North Mankato, MN.

Table of Contents

What Is Precipitation?

Plants, animals, and people all need water to live.

The **water cycle** moves water to the earth from the sky. Precipitation is part of this cycle.

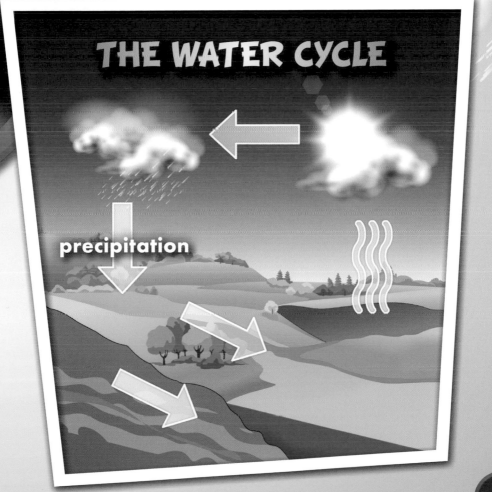

THE WATER CYCLE

precipitation

Precipitation is water that falls
from clouds.

It can fall as a **liquid** or a **solid**.

Rain is a liquid form. It can come as a **sprinkle** or a **downpour**.

Drizzle is a misty liquid. It is finer than rain.

Precipitation becomes snow
when weather is colder.

The solid flakes can be wet and sticky or light and powdery.

Sometimes precipitation is a mix of rain and snow. It can also fall as small bits of ice called **sleet**.

Freezing rain happens when water droplets become ice when they land.

Hail happens during **severe weather**. It falls as hard balls of ice.

Hail can be small like peas or large like softballs. It can dent cars and houses.

Meteorologists use **radar** to locate precipitation.

radar

Radar shows where rain and snow will be. It tells how much might fall.

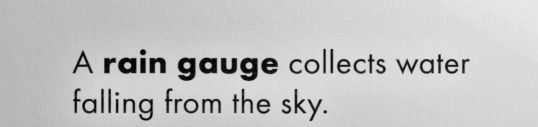

A **rain gauge** collects water falling from the sky.

The measurement shows how much water has fallen.

Farmers need just the right amount of precipitation. Too much causes **flooding**.

Too little means a **drought**.
Crops cannot grow without water!

Glossary

downpour—a heavy rain

drizzle—gentle, misty rain

drought—a long period of dry weather

flooding—water covering land that is usually dry

freezing rain—water droplets that freeze when they hit objects or the ground

hail—hard balls of ice; hail falls during severe weather.

liquid—a substance that flows

meteorologists—people who study and predict the weather

radar—a tool that sends out radio waves to collect weather data

rain gauge—a tool used to collect and measure precipitation

severe weather—bad weather that can harm land, buildings, and people

sleet—small bits of ice; sleet falls in colder weather.

solid—a substance with an exact shape

sprinkle—a light rain

water cycle—the process in which water falls from the sky, collects in bodies of water, and returns to the air

To Learn More

AT THE LIBRARY

Edison, Erin. *Rain*. Mankato, Minn.: Capstone Press, 2012.

Johnson, Robin. *What Is Precipitation?* St. Catharines, Ont.: Crabtree Publishing Company, 2013.

Mezzanotte, Jim. *Hailstorms*. Pleasantville, N.Y.: Weekly Reader Pub., 2010.

ON THE WEB

Learning more about precipitation is as easy as 1, 2, 3.

1. Go to www.factsurfer.com.

2. Enter "precipitation" into the search box.

3. Click the "Surf" button and you will see a list of related web sites.

With factsurfer.com, finding more information is just a click away.

Index

The images in this book are reproduced through the courtesy of: Patrick Foto, front cover; solarseven, weather symbols (front cover, all interior pages); KPG_Payless, pp. 2-3 (background); Marilyn Nieves, p. 4; ArtMari, p. 5; AJancso, pp. 6-7; Terraxplorer, p. 8; gpointstudio, p. 9; emholk, p. 10; BlueSkyImage, p. 11; Associated Press, pp. 12, 14, 17; Hyungwon Kang/ Reuters/ Corbis, p. 13; Suzanne Tucker, p. 15; Gene Blevins/ Corbis, p. 16; thieury, p. 18; Roland Magnusson, p. 19; Dave Reede/ All Canada Photos/ Superstock, p. 20; Nic Bothma/ EPA/ Newscom, p. 21.